Recipe Collection

BAKING

Publications International Ltd.

Favorite Brand Name Recipes at www.fbnr.com

Recipes developed and tested by Land O'Lakes Test Kitchens. For questions regarding recipes in this cookbook or LAND O LAKES® products, call 1-800-328-4155.

Special thanks to the staff of Land O'Lakes, Inc., including Amy Jeatran, Publisher; Becky Wahlund, Director of Test Kitchens; Marge Ryerson, Editor; and Pat Weed, Publications Coordinator.

Pictured on the front cover: Sour Cream Cherry Scones (page 25).

Pictured on the back cover: Cornmeal Skillet Rolls (page 19), Crumb Top Rhubarb Pie (page 59), Raspberry Cheesecake with Chocolate Crust (page 36).

ISBN-13: 978-1-4127-2673-3
ISBN-10: 1-4127-2673-5

Manufactured in China.

8 7 6 5 4 3 2 1

Preparation and Cooking Times: All recipes were developed and tested in the Land O'Lakes Test Kitchens by professional home economists. Use "Preparation Time" and "Cooking, Baking, Microwaving or Broiling Time" given with each recipe as guides. Preparation time is based on the approximate amount of "active" time required to assemble the recipe. This includes steps such as chopping, mixing, cooking pasta, frosting, etc. Cooking, baking, microwaving or broiling times are based on the minimum amount of time required for these recipe steps.

CONTENTS

28

50

72

68

BAKING

It's better with butter

Nothing equals the wonderful flavor of real butter and the homemade goodness it adds to baked goods. When you bake, butter plays a major role in tenderizing, adding flavor and color, and helping baked goods to brown. Here are some tips for better baking with butter:

What is the best way to soften butter? Soften butter for easier mixing by removing it from the refrigerator and letting it stand 30 to 45 minutes at room temperature. In a hurry? Cut butter into chunks and let stand 15 minutes at room temperature, or place a stick of cold butter between sheets of waxed paper and smash it on both sides with a rolling pin. We don't recommend softening butter in the microwave because it can melt too quickly.

Can salted and unsalted butter be substituted for one another? Salted and unsalted butter may be substituted for one another without altering the amount of salt in the recipe. Unsalted butter gives recipes a delicate, cultured flavor.

How long can I store my butter? Always refrigerate butter in the original packaging, including its original wrapper, and store in the coldest part of the refrigerator—not in the "butter keeper" in the door. Butter will retain its freshness for four months. For longer storage, place carton in a plastic bag or wrap in aluminum foil and freeze.

12

15

34

Measuring Tips

Butter: Cut sticks as marked on the wrapper, using a sharp knife.

Cup	Equivalent Measure(s)
1 cup	2 sticks or ½ pound
⅔ cup	10 tablespoons plus 2 teaspoons
½ cup	1 stick or ¼ pound
⅓ cup	5 tablespoons plus 1 teaspoon
¼ cup	½ stick or 4 tablespoons

Flour: Stir flour with a large spoon to loosen it up. Lightly spoon flour into a dry measuring cup and level top with a spatula or knife. Do not tap or shake the measuring cup when measuring, or you will get too much flour. Sifting isn't necessary unless the recipe specifically calls for it.

Brown sugar: Pack firmly into dry measuring cup until level with top.

Cornmeal, granulated sugar, oats, and powdered sugar: Spoon into a dry measuring cup and level top with a spatula or knife.

Leavenings and spices: Fill a standard measuring spoon to the top and level with a spatula or knife.

Liquids: A common baking mistake is measuring liquid ingredients in dry measuring cups. All liquids—including milk, honey, corn syrup—should be poured into a glass or clear plastic liquid measuring cup on a level surface. Bend down so your eye is level with the marking on the cup for an accurate reading. For easy removal of sticky liquids such as corn syrup, honey, or molasses, spray the measuring cup first with cooking spray.

The Basic Tools

- Bread (loaf) pans 9×5×3 or 8×4×3-inch
- Cake pans 13×9-inch, 8- or 9-inch square, 9-inch round, 12-cup Bundt®, 9-inch springform, or 10-inch tube pan
- Cookie sheets approximately 14×17-inch, shiny aluminum without sides
- Jelly-roll pan 15×10×1-inch
- Muffin pan 12-cup
- Cookie and/or biscuit cutters
- Electric hand-held or stand-up mixer
- Kitchen timer
- Measuring cups and spoons
- Metal spatula or turner
- Mixing bowls
- Rolling pin
- Rubber spatula
- Wooden spoons
- Cooling racks

60

84

86

Best-Loved Blueberry Muffins, p. 12

Cornmeal Skillet Rolls
(opposite page), p. 19

BREADS &
QUICK BREADS

Breads and quick breads are so much more than just loaves and muffins (although we love those recipes, too). Try some of these biscuits and scones to start your day off right. Or try these rolls and buns, which are perfect for extraordinary sandwiches or to round out a meal.

Nutmeg Streusel Muffins

Preparation time: **10 minutes** | Baking time: **18 minutes** | 1 dozen muffins

Streusel

1⅓ cups all-purpose flour
  1 cup firmly packed brown sugar
  ½ cup cold LAND O LAKES® Butter

Muffins

  ⅔ cup all-purpose flour
  ⅔ cup buttermilk*
  1 egg
1½ teaspoons baking powder
1½ teaspoons ground nutmeg
  ½ teaspoon baking soda
  ½ teaspoon salt

• Heat oven to 400°F. Combine 1⅓ cups flour and brown sugar in large bowl; cut in butter with pastry blender or fork until mixture resembles coarse crumbs. Reserve ½ cup.

• Add all muffin ingredients to remaining streusel mixture in same bowl; stir just until moistened.

• Spoon batter into greased or paper-lined 12-cup muffin pan. Sprinkle each with reserved streusel. Bake for 18 to 22 minutes or until lightly browned. Let stand 5 minutes; remove from pan.

*Substitute 2 teaspoons vinegar or lemon juice and enough milk to equal ⅔ cup. Let stand 10 minutes.

Chocolate Toffee Brunch Biscuits

Preparation time: **15 minutes** | Baking time: **15 minutes** | **12 biscuits**

    2 cups all-purpose flour
    ¼ cup sugar
    2 teaspoons baking powder
    ¼ teaspoon baking soda
    ½ cup cold LAND O LAKES® Butter
    ¾ cup milk
    ¼ cup mini real semi-sweet chocolate chips
    ¼ cup almond or English toffee bits

    2 tablespoons LAND O LAKES® Butter, melted
    1 tablespoon sugar

• Heat oven to 375°F. Combine flour, ¼ cup sugar, baking powder and baking soda in large bowl; cut in ½ cup butter with pastry blender or fork until mixture resembles coarse crumbs. Stir in milk just until flour is moistened. Gently stir in chocolate chips and toffee bits.

• Drop about ¼ cup batter for each biscuit, 1 inch apart, onto large ungreased baking sheet. Brush tops with melted butter. Sprinkle biscuits evenly with 1 tablespoon sugar. Bake for 15 to 20 minutes or until lightly browned. Serve warm.

Best-Loved Blueberry Muffins

Preparation time: **15 minutes** | Baking time: **22 minutes** | **1 dozen muffins**

Muffin

1   cup milk
½   cup LAND O LAKES® Butter, melted
1   egg, slightly beaten
2   cups all-purpose flour
⅓   cup sugar
2   teaspoons baking powder
1   teaspoon salt
1   cup fresh or frozen blueberries

Topping

¼   cup LAND O LAKES® Butter, melted
¼   cup sugar

• Heat oven to 375°F. Combine milk, ½ cup melted butter and egg in large bowl. Add all remaining muffin ingredients except blueberries; stir just until moistened. Gently stir in blueberries.

• Spoon batter into greased or paper-lined 12-cup muffin pan. Bake for 22 to 26 minutes or until golden brown. Cool slightly; remove from pan.

• Dip tops of muffins in ¼ cup melted butter, then in sugar.

variations:
Lemon Blueberry Muffins: Prepare muffins as directed, stirring in 1 tablespoon freshly grated lemon peel with flour. Bake as directed.
Raspberry-White Chocolate Chip Muffins: Omit blueberries. Add 1 cup fresh or frozen raspberries for blueberries. Gently stir in ½ cup white baking chips with raspberries.

tip:
Muffins can also be baked in nonstick Texas-size muffin pan. Bake for 27 to 32 minutes. Makes 6 muffins.

Swedish Rye Bread

Preparation time: **15 minutes** | Baking time: **25 minutes** | **12 servings (2 loaves)**

    ¾ cup warm (105°F to 115°F) water
    1 (16-ounce) package hot roll mix
    2 eggs
    2 tablespoons LAND O LAKES® Butter, softened
    2 tablespoons mild-flavored molasses
    ¾ cup rye flour
    1 teaspoon freshly grated orange peel
    1 teaspoon fennel or caraway seeds, if desired

• Combine water and yeast from hot roll mix in small bowl; stir to dissolve. Stir in eggs, butter and molasses.

• Combine dry mixture from hot roll mix, rye flour, orange peel and fennel seeds in large bowl; add yeast mixture. Stir until soft dough forms. Turn dough out onto lightly floured surface; knead until smooth, adding all-purpose flour, if necessary, to reduce stickiness (3 to 5 minutes).

• Divide dough in half; shape each half into round 6-inch circle. Place loaves onto greased baking sheet. Cover; let rise in warm place until double in size (45 to 60 minutes).

• Heat oven to 350°F. Make diagonal cuts in top of loaves with sharp knife just before baking. Bake for 25 to 30 minutes or until golden brown and loaves sound hollow when tapped.

Mini Poppy Seed Muffins

Preparation time: **25 minutes** | Baking time: **15 minutes** | **3 dozen mini muffins**

    1⅓ cups all-purpose flour
     2 tablespoons poppy seed
     ½ teaspoon baking powder
     ¼ teaspoon baking soda
     ⅛ teaspoon salt
     ¾ cup sugar
     ⅔ cup LAND O LAKES® Butter, softened
     2 eggs
     1 teaspoon vanilla
     ¼ teaspoon lemon extract, if desired
     ⅓ cup lemon yogurt

• Heat oven to 350°F. Line 36 mini muffin cups with paper liners. Combine flour, poppy seed, baking powder, baking soda and salt in medium bowl. Set aside.

• Combine sugar and butter in large bowl. Beat at medium speed, scraping bowl often, until creamy. Add eggs, one at a time, beating well after each addition. Add vanilla and lemon extract; mix well. Reduce speed to low; alternately add flour mixture and yogurt, beating well after each addition, just until moistened.

• Spoon batter into prepared mini muffin cups. Bake for 15 to 18 minutes or until set and very lightly browned.

Oat Bran Popovers with Herb Butter

Preparation time: **15 minutes** | Baking time: **35 minutes** | 6 popovers; ⅓ cup Herb Butter

Herb Butter

⅓ cup LAND O LAKES® Butter, softened
1 teaspoon finely chopped fresh oregano leaves*
1 teaspoon chopped fresh parsley

Popovers

3 eggs
1¼ cups milk
1 tablespoon LAND O LAKES® Butter, melted
1 cup all-purpose flour
¼ cup oat bran
¼ teaspoon salt

• Heat oven to 450°F. Stir together ⅓ cup butter, oregano and parsley in small bowl. Cover; refrigerate until serving time.

• Beat eggs in small bowl at medium speed, scraping bowl often, until thick and lemon-colored. Add milk and 1 tablespoon butter; continue beating 1 minute. Add flour, oat bran and salt; continue beating until well mixed. Pour batter into well-greased popover pan or 6-ounce custard cups. Bake for 15 minutes.

• Reduce oven temperature to 350°F. (DO NOT OPEN OVEN DOOR.) Bake for 20 to 25 minutes or until golden brown.

• Insert knife into popovers to allow steam to escape. Serve immediately with Herb Butter.

*Substitute ½ teaspoon dried oregano leaves, crushed.

tip:
Eggs and milk should be at room temperature to help ensure successful popovers.

Everyone's Favorite Buns

Preparation time: **30 minutes** | Baking time: **14 minutes** | **24 buns**

  ½ cup milk
  6 tablespoons LAND O LAKES® Butter
     Warm water (105°F to 115°F)
  ½ cup sugar
  1 egg
  1 teaspoon salt
  2 (¼-ounce) packages active dry yeast
  5 to 5½ cups bread flour

• Place milk and 4 tablespoons butter in 2-cup glass measuring cup. Microwave on HIGH for 1½ minutes. Add enough warm water to measure 2 cups.

• Combine sugar, egg and salt in large bowl; mix well. Add milk mixture; mix well. Stir in yeast; let stand 2 minutes.

• Add 3 cups flour. Beat at medium speed, scraping bowl often, until smooth and elastic. Add 2 cups flour. Mix dough with hook or stir in by hand until smooth. Stir in enough remaining flour by hand to make dough easy to handle.

• Place dough into greased bowl. Melt remaining 2 tablespoons butter; brush top of dough. Reserve remaining melted butter. Cover; let rise in warm place until double in size (about 45 minutes). (Dough is ready if indentation remains when touched.)

• Punch down dough; divide in half. Shape each half on lightly floured surface into 12 buns. Place buns onto two parchment-lined or greased 15×10×1-inch jelly-roll pans. Brush with reserved melted butter. Cover; let rise in warm place until double in size (about 1 hour).

• Heat oven to 375°F. Bake for 14 to 16 minutes or until golden brown. Remove from pan immediately. Brush buns with reserved melted butter, if desired.

Coconut Cherry Scones with Citrus Butter

Preparation time: **20 minutes** | Baking time: **20 minutes** | 8 scones; ½ cup Citrus Butter

Citrus Butter
- ½ cup LAND O LAKES® Butter, softened
- 1 tablespoon powdered sugar
- 1 teaspoon freshly grated lemon peel
- 1 teaspoon freshly grated orange peel

Scones
- 2 cups all-purpose flour
- ¼ cup sugar
- 2½ teaspoons baking powder
- ¼ teaspoon salt
- ½ cup cold LAND O LAKES® Butter
- 1 egg, beaten
- ½ cup LAND O LAKES™ Half & Half
- ⅓ cup sweetened flaked coconut
- ½ cup dried cherries or sweetened dried cranberries, chopped
- 1 teaspoon freshly grated lemon peel
- 1 tablespoon coarse grain or decorator sugar

• Heat oven to 375°F. Combine all citrus butter ingredients in small bowl. Beat at low speed, scraping bowl often, until creamy. Set aside.

• Combine flour, sugar, baking powder and salt in medium bowl; cut in ½ cup butter with pastry blender or fork until mixture resembles coarse crumbs. Combine egg, half & half, coconut, cherries and lemon peel in small bowl. Add to flour mixture. Stir just until flour mixture is moistened.

• Turn dough onto lightly floured surface; knead lightly 8 to 10 times. Pat dough into 7-inch circle. Place onto greased baking sheet. Cut into 8 wedges. (Do not separate.) Sprinkle with coarse sugar. Bake for 20 to 25 minutes or until golden brown. Cool 15 minutes. Cut wedges apart; remove from baking sheet. Serve warm scones with citrus butter.

Cornmeal Skillet Rolls

Preparation time: **20 minutes** | Baking time: **30 minutes** | **16 rolls**

    1 cup boiling water
    ½ cup cornmeal
    ¼ cup mild-flavored molasses
    3 tablespoons LAND O LAKES®
      Butter
    1 teaspoon salt
    1 egg
    ¼ cup warm water (105°F to 115°F)
    1 (¼-ounce) package active dry yeast
    3 cups all-purpose flour
    1 tablespoon LAND O LAKES® Butter,
      melted

• Place boiling water in small bowl.
Slowly add cornmeal, stirring constantly,
until well mixed. Add molasses,
3 tablespoons butter and salt. Stir until
butter is melted. Stir in egg; mix well. Set
aside.

• Combine warm water and yeast in
another small bowl. Stir until yeast is
dissolved.

• Place flour in large bowl. Add cornmeal
and yeast mixtures; stir until soft dough
forms. Turn dough onto well-floured surface. Knead with well-floured hands until ball forms (1 to
2 minutes). (Dough will be sticky.) Cut dough into 16 pieces with sharp knife.

• Shape each piece of dough into ball with well-floured hands. Place balls into greased 10-inch
cast iron skillet or 9-inch round baking pan. Cover; let rise in warm place until double in size (30 to
45 minutes).

• Heat oven to 375°F. Bake for 30 to 35 minutes or until golden brown and rolls sound hollow when
tapped. Remove from pan; cool on wire rack. Brush with 1 tablespoon melted butter. Serve warm.

tip:
Yeast must be activated by dissolving in warm water. The liquid should be from 105°F to 115°F. If the
water is too warm, the yeast will be killed and the dough will not rise. Use a thermometer to
determine if the water is at a safe temperature to dissolve yeast. Do not use packages of yeast
that are older than their expiration date.

Orange Praline Quick Bread

Preparation time: **20 minutes** | Baking time: **30 minutes** | **32 servings (4 mini loaves)**

Bread

  1 cup sugar
  1 cup LAND O LAKES® Sour Cream
  ½ cup LAND O LAKES® Butter, softened
  2 eggs
  1 tablespoon freshly grated orange peel
  1 teaspoon vanilla
  2 cups all-purpose flour
  2 teaspoons baking powder
  ½ teaspoon baking soda
  ½ teaspoon salt
  1 cup chopped pecans

Glaze

  ⅓ cup firmly packed brown sugar
  ⅓ cup LAND O LAKES® Butter
  ¼ cup finely chopped pecans

• Heat oven to 350°F. Combine sugar, sour cream, butter, eggs, orange peel and vanilla in large bowl. Beat at medium speed, scraping bowl often, until well mixed. Reduce speed to low; add flour, baking powder, baking soda and salt. Beat just until moistened. Stir in 1 cup pecans.

• Spoon batter evenly into four greased mini 5½×3-inch loaf pans. Bake for 30 to 35 minutes or until toothpick inserted in center comes out clean. Cool 10 minutes; remove from pans.

• Meanwhile, combine brown sugar and ⅓ cup butter in 1-quart saucepan. Cook over medium heat until mixture comes to a boil (3 to 4 minutes). Spoon glaze mixture over warm loaves. Immediately sprinkle with ¼ cup pecans.

tip:
Substitute one (9×5-inch) greased loaf pan. Bake for 60 to 65 minutes.

tip:
Serve bread with maple-flavored butter. Combine ⅓ cup softened LAND O LAKES® Butter, ¼ cup orange marmalade and 1 tablespoon maple syrup; mix well.

Berry Twist Bread

Preparation time: **25 minutes** | Baking time: **20 minutes** | **16 servings (1 loaf)**

Bread

- ½ cup warm milk (105°F to 115°F)
- ⅓ cup warm water (105°F to 115°F)
- 1 (¼-ounce) package active dry yeast
- 3 to 3½ cups all-purpose flour
- ¼ cup sugar
- ¼ cup LAND O LAKES® Butter, melted
- 1 egg
- 1⅛ teaspoons salt
- 2 tablespoons seedless raspberry jam

Glaze

- ¾ cup powdered sugar
- 1 to 2 tablespoons orange juice
- 1 teaspoon freshly grated orange peel, if desired

• Combine warm milk and water in large bowl; add yeast. Stir to dissolve. Stir in 2¾ cups flour, sugar, butter, egg and 1 teaspoon salt until soft dough forms.

• Turn dough out onto lightly floured surface. Knead dough, adding additional flour 1 tablespoon at a time, if necessary, until dough is smooth (5 to 10 minutes). Place dough into greased bowl; turn greased-side up. Cover; let rise in warm place until double in size (45 to 60 minutes).

• Knead dough on lightly floured surface (30 seconds). Cover; let rest 10 minutes.

• Roll dough into 15×10-inch rectangle. Combine jam and ⅛ teaspoon salt in small bowl. Spread dough with jam mixture to within ½ inch of edge. Roll up, beginning with 15-inch side. Place onto large greased baking sheet. Form into circle; pinch ends to seal. Cut ¾ of the way through dough every 1½ inches on outside edge with kitchen shears or serrated knife. Twist each section of dough, turning it on side to form ring. Cover; let rise in warm place until double in size (30 to 45 minutes).

• Heat oven to 350°F. Bake for 20 to 30 minutes or until golden brown. Remove from pan; cool completely on wire rack.

• Meanwhile, combine powdered sugar, 1 tablespoon orange juice and orange peel, if desired, in small bowl. Add enough additional orange juice for desired glazing consistency. Drizzle over cooled bread.

Veggie Garden Bread

Preparation time: **15 minutes** | Baking time: **30 minutes** | **12 servings (1½-pound loaf)**

1   cup warm water (105°F to 115°F)
1   (¼-ounce) package active dry yeast
½   cup finely shredded carrot
2   tablespoons LAND O LAKES® Butter, softened
1   tablespoon firmly packed brown sugar
2   teaspoons dried minced onion
2   teaspoons chopped fresh rosemary*
1½ teaspoons salt
2¾ to 3¼ cups bread flour

• Pour water into large bowl; add yeast. Stir to dissolve. Stir in carrot, butter, brown sugar, onion, rosemary and salt. Stir in 2¾ cups flour until soft dough forms.

• Turn dough out onto lightly floured surface. Knead dough, adding additional bread flour 1 tablespoon at a time, if necessary, until dough is smooth (5 to 10 minutes). Place dough into greased bowl; turn greased-side up. Cover; let rise in warm place until double in size (45 to 60 minutes).

• Punch down dough; shape into loaf. Place into greased 9×5-inch loaf pan. Cover; let rise in warm place until double in size (30 to 45 minutes).

• Heat oven to 375°F. Bake for 30 to 35 minutes or until loaf sounds hollow when tapped.

*Substitute ¾ teaspoon dried rosemary.

variation:

Bread machine directions for 1½-pound loaf: Omit active dry yeast. Substitute 1½ teaspoons bread machine yeast, water at room temperature and use 3 cups bread flour. Read instruction manual of your bread machine. Prepare bread according to manual directions for basic or white bread setting. During the mixing cycle, check the dough. The dough may seem too wet or too dry, depending upon the moisture content of the carrots, moisture content of the flour and humidity. If the dough is sticky, add more flour, 1 tablespoon at a time, until the dough is smooth and soft. If the dough is firm or the bread machine is having difficulty mixing it, add water, 1 teaspoon at a time, until the dough is smooth and soft.

Sour Cream Cherry Scones

Preparation time: **20 minutes** | Baking time: **25 minutes** | **16 scones**

Topping
¼ cup sliced almonds
1 tablespoon sugar

Scones
2½ cups all-purpose flour
½ cup sugar
2 teaspoons baking powder
½ teaspoon salt
½ cup LAND O LAKES® Butter, softened
¾ cup LAND O LAKES® Sour Cream
1 egg
½ teaspoon almond extract
⅔ cup dried cherries*

• Heat oven to 375°F. Combine all topping ingredients in small bowl; mix well. Set aside.

• Combine flour, sugar, baking powder and salt in large bowl; cut in butter with pastry blender or fork until mixture resembles coarse crumbs.

• Combine sour cream, egg and almond extract in small bowl until smooth. Stir into flour mixture just until moistened. Stir in cherries.

• Turn dough onto lightly floured surface; knead 8 to 10 times until smooth, adding small amount of flour, if necessary.

• Divide dough in half. Pat each half into a 7-inch circle. Place 2 inches apart onto large ungreased baking sheet. Sprinkle topping evenly over dough. Score each half into 8 wedges; do not separate. Bake for 25 to 30 minutes or until scones are lightly browned. Cool 15 minutes; separate scones. Store leftover scones in airtight container at room temperature.

*Substitute ⅔ cup sweetened dried cranberries.

tip:
Coarsely chop cherries if they are large.

Mini Pineapple Ginger Upside-Down Cakes, p. 32

Raspberry Cheesecake with Chocolate Crust
(opposite page), p. 36

CAKES &
CHEESECAKES

These great-tasting cakes and cheesecakes are just right for any gathering, whatever the reason for getting together. They are sure to make your next party a real celebration!

Mocha Chocolate Cheesecake

Preparation time: **30 minutes** | Baking time: **50 minutes** | **12 servings**

Crust

1⅓ cups graham cracker crumbs

¼ cup LAND O LAKES® Butter, melted

2 tablespoons sugar

Filling

1 cup sugar

½ cup LAND O LAKES® Sour Cream

3 (8-ounce) packages cream cheese, softened

3 tablespoons all-purpose flour

3 eggs

1 tablespoon vanilla

2 teaspoons instant coffee granules

1 tablespoon hot water

¼ cup unsweetened cocoa

3 tablespoons LAND O LAKES® Butter, melted

Garnish

1 (1.4-ounce) English toffee bar, chopped

• Heat oven to 325°F. Stir together all crust ingredients in medium bowl. Press crumb mixture evenly onto bottom of ungreased 9-inch springform pan. Bake for 10 minutes or until golden brown. Cool completely.

• Meanwhile, combine ¾ cup sugar, sour cream, cream cheese and flour in large bowl. Beat at low speed, scraping bowl often, until creamy. Add eggs and vanilla; continue beating until well mixed. Reserve 1½ cups cream cheese mixture. Set aside.

• Combine coffee granules and water in small bowl; stir until granules dissolve. Combine remaining ¼ cup sugar, cocoa and 3 tablespoons melted butter in small bowl; stir until smooth. Add coffee and cocoa mixtures to remaining cream cheese mixture; continue beating until well mixed. Pour cocoa-cream cheese mixture over baked crust. Spoon reserved cream cheese mixture over chocolate mixture; pull knife through batter for marbled effect.

• Bake for 50 to 60 minutes or until set 2 inches from edge of pan. (Center will still be soft.) Remove from oven; let stand 10 minutes. Loosen sides of cheesecake from pan by carefully running knife around inside of pan. (Dip knife in hot water if cheesecake sticks to knife.) Do not remove sides. Cool 1 hour. Cover; refrigerate at least 4 hours. Remove sides of pan.

• To serve, garnish with chopped English toffee bar. Store refrigerated.

Lemon Snack Cake

Preparation time: **15 minutes** | Baking time: **30 minutes** | **8 servings**

Cake

1¼ cups all-purpose flour
1 cup sugar
1½ teaspoons baking powder
½ teaspoon salt
1 egg
2 teaspoons freshly grated lemon peel
¼ cup LAND O LAKES® Butter, melted
¾ cup milk

Glaze

¾ cup powdered sugar
1 tablespoon LAND O LAKES® Butter, melted
2 to 3 teaspoons lemon juice

• Heat oven to 350°F. Combine flour, sugar, baking powder and salt in lightly greased 8-inch square baking pan. Make 2 indentations in flour mixture. Set aside.

• Combine egg and lemon peel in small bowl with fork; pour into 1 indentation. Pour ¼ cup melted butter in other indentation. Pour milk over all; mix well. (Some lumps will remain.)

• Bake for 30 to 35 minutes or until toothpick inserted in center comes out clean. Cool completely.

• Combine powdered sugar, 1 tablespoon melted butter and enough lemon juice for desired glazing consistency in small bowl. Spread glaze over cooled cake.

Mini Pineapple Ginger Upside-Down Cakes

Preparation time: **20 minutes** | Baking time: **20 minutes** | **12 mini cakes**

Topping

½ cup firmly packed brown sugar

1 (8-ounce) can pineapple tidbits, well-drained

3 tablespoons LAND O LAKES® Butter, melted

Cakes

1⅓ cups all-purpose flour

½ cup firmly packed brown sugar

1 teaspoon baking powder

1 teaspoon ground ginger

½ teaspoon salt

¼ teaspoon baking soda

¼ cup LAND O LAKES® Butter, melted

1 (8-ounce) container plain yogurt

1 egg, beaten

LAND O LAKES™ Heavy Whipping Cream, whipped, if desired

Maraschino cherries, if desired

• Heat oven to 375°F. Combine all topping ingredients in small bowl. Place 1 tablespoon topping mixture into each greased 1¼-inch deep muffin cup.

• Combine flour, brown sugar, baking powder, ginger, salt and baking soda in large bowl. Add ¼ cup butter, yogurt and egg; mix well.

• Spoon batter over topping mixture in muffin cups. Bake for 20 to 25 minutes or until tops are golden brown. Cool 3 minutes. Immediately turn onto serving plate. Serve warm. Top with whipped cream and cherry, if desired.

tip:

Baking soda, in addition to baking powder, is used for leavening quick breads that include acidic ingredients such as brown sugar, molasses, yogurt, sour cream or buttermilk. The alkaline baking soda reacts with these acidic ingredients to create bubbles of carbon dioxide, causing the batter to rise.

tip:

If using shallow muffin pan, recipe will make 15 mini cakes. Bake for 15 to 20 minutes or until tops are golden brown.

Rhubarb Cookie Cake

Preparation time: **15 minutes** | Baking time: **40 minutes** | **9 servings**

Crust
½ cup LAND O LAKES® Butter
1 cup all-purpose flour
⅓ cup sugar

Filling
2 cups sliced fresh rhubarb*
⅔ cup sugar
¼ cup all-purpose flour
¾ teaspoon baking powder
½ teaspoon ground ginger
2 eggs
¼ cup firmly packed brown sugar

Topping
1 cup LAND O LAKES™ Heavy Whipping Cream
2 tablespoons firmly packed brown sugar

• Heat oven to 350°F. Melt butter in 2-quart saucepan over medium-low heat. Cook, stirring constantly, until butter just begins to turn golden brown (3 to 4 minutes). Immediately remove from heat. Add 1 cup flour and ⅓ cup sugar; mix well. Press firmly onto bottom of ungreased 8-inch square baking pan.

• Combine rhubarb, ⅔ cup sugar, ¼ cup flour, baking powder and ginger in medium bowl. Beat in eggs with wooden spoon until smooth; pour over crust. Sprinkle ¼ cup brown sugar evenly over top. Bake for 40 to 45 minutes or until top is golden brown and toothpick inserted in center comes out clean. Cool at least 30 minutes before cutting.

• Combine whipping cream and 2 tablespoons brown sugar in small bowl. Beat at high speed until soft peaks form. Dollop each serving with sweetened whipped cream.

*Substitute 2 cups frozen rhubarb, thawed and patted dry with paper towels.

Raspberry Cheesecake with Chocolate Crust

Preparation time: **40 minutes** | Baking time: **1 hour** | **12 servings**

Filling

1 (10-ounce) package frozen raspberries, partially thawed

1 tablespoon cornstarch

Crust

1 (9-ounce) package chocolate wafer cookies

⅓ cup LAND O LAKES® Butter, melted

Cheesecake

1½ cups sugar

2 (8-ounce) packages cream cheese, softened

4 eggs

1½ cups LAND O LAKES® Sour Cream

3 tablespoons cornstarch

1 teaspoon vanilla

Glaze

2 (1-ounce) squares semi-sweet baking chocolate

¼ cup water

2 tablespoons LAND O LAKES® Butter

• Combine raspberries and 1 tablespoon cornstarch in 2-quart saucepan. Cook over medium heat, stirring constantly, until mixture comes to a boil (6 to 10 minutes). Continue boiling 1 minute. Remove from heat. Cool 10 minutes.

• Heat oven to 325°F. Place cookies in food processor bowl fitted with metal blade. Cover; process until very finely chopped (30 to 40 seconds). Add melted butter; process until smooth (20 to 30 seconds). Press onto bottom of 9-inch springform pan; set aside.

• Combine sugar and cream cheese in large bowl. Beat at medium speed, scraping bowl often, until creamy. Add eggs, 1 at a time, beating well after each addition. Add sour cream and 3 tablespoons cornstarch. Continue beating, scraping bowl often, until well mixed. Stir in vanilla.

• Pour half of cheesecake batter over crust. Spoon filling evenly over batter in pan. Top with remaining cheesecake batter. Bake for 60 to 70 minutes or until just set 2 inches from edge of pan. Turn off oven; leave cheesecake in oven 2 hours. Remove from oven; loosen sides of cheesecake from pan by running knife around inside of pan. Cool completely (about 2 hours). Loosely cover; refrigerate 8 hours or overnight.

• Combine all glaze ingredients in 1-quart saucepan. Cook over medium heat, stirring occasionally, until chocolate and butter are melted and glaze is smooth.

• To serve, cut into individual servings; place onto serving plates. Drizzle about 1 tablespoon glaze over each serving. Store refrigerated.

Rocky Road Chocolate Cake

Preparation time: **20 minutes** | Baking time: **32 minutes** | **15 servings**

Cake

- 2 cups all-purpose flour
- 1½ cups sugar
- 1 cup water
- ½ cup unsweetened cocoa
- ½ cup LAND O LAKES® Butter, softened
- 3 eggs
- 1¼ teaspoons baking powder
- 1 teaspoon baking soda
- 1 teaspoon vanilla

Frosting

- 2 cups miniature marshmallows
- ¼ cup LAND O LAKES® Butter
- 1 (3-ounce) package cream cheese
- 1 (1-ounce) square unsweetened baking chocolate
- 2 tablespoons milk
- 3 cups powdered sugar
- 1 teaspoon vanilla
- ½ cup coarsely chopped salted peanuts

• Heat oven to 350°F. Combine all cake ingredients in large bowl. Beat at low speed, scraping bowl often, until moistened. Increase speed to high. Beat, scraping bowl often, until smooth.

• Pour batter into greased and floured 13×9-inch baking pan. Bake for 30 to 40 minutes or until toothpick inserted in center comes out clean. Sprinkle with marshmallows. Continue baking 2 minutes or until marshmallows are softened.

• Meanwhile, combine ¼ cup butter, cream cheese, chocolate and milk in 2-quart saucepan. Cook over medium heat, stirring occasionally, until melted (8 to 10 minutes). Remove from heat; stir in powdered sugar and 1 teaspoon vanilla until smooth. Pour over marshmallows and swirl together. Sprinkle with peanuts.

Sensational Irish Cream Cheesecake

Preparation time: **30 minutes** | Baking time: **45 minutes** | **16 servings**

Crust
1¾ cups finely crushed chocolate graham crackers
6 tablespoons LAND O LAKES® Butter, melted

Filling
1 cup sugar
3 (8-ounce) packages cream cheese, softened
4 eggs
⅓ to ½ cup Irish cream liqueur*
¾ cup mini real semi-sweet chocolate chips
1 teaspoon all-purpose flour

Garnish
LAND O LAKES™ Heavy Whipping Cream, whipped, if desired
Chocolate curls, if desired

• Heat oven to 375°F. Combine all crust ingredients in medium bowl. Press onto bottom and 1 inch up sides of lightly greased 9-inch springform pan. Set aside.

• Combine sugar and cream cheese in large bowl. Beat at medium speed, scraping bowl often, until creamy. Add eggs, 1 at a time, beating well after each addition. (DO NOT OVERBEAT.) Stir in liqueur.

• Combine ½ cup chocolate chips and flour in small bowl; gently stir into cream cheese mixture. Pour batter over crust. Sprinkle remaining chocolate chips over batter.

• Bake for 45 to 55 minutes or until center is set and firm to touch. Cool 10 minutes. Loosen side of cheesecake by running knife around inside of pan. Cover; refrigerate at least 3 hours.

• Pipe or spoon whipped cream over edge of cheesecake and top with chocolate curls, if desired. Store refrigerated.

*Substitute ¼ cup LAND O LAKES™ Half & Half or milk, 2 tablespoons cooled coffee and 1 teaspoon almond extract.

Chocolate Caramel Cheesecake Bites

Preparation time: **1 hour** | Baking time: **35 minutes** | **36 bites**

Crust
¾ cup chocolate cookie crumbs

3 tablespoons LAND O LAKES® Butter, melted

Filling
20 caramels, unwrapped

¼ cup LAND O LAKES™ Fat Free Half & Half

⅓ cup chopped pecans, toasted

1 (8-ounce) package cream cheese, softened

⅓ cup sugar

1 egg

½ teaspoon vanilla

¼ cup LAND O LAKES® Sour Cream

Coating
1 (12-ounce) package (2 cups) real semi-sweet chocolate chips

½ cup shortening

• Heat oven to 350°F. Line 8-inch square baking pan with double thickness of aluminum foil, extending foil over ends of pan. Spray foil with no-stick cooking spray. Combine all crust ingredients in small bowl. Press onto bottom of prepared pan.

• Combine caramels and half & half in medium microwave-safe bowl. Microwave on HIGH 1 minute; stir. Continue microwaving 30 seconds; stir until smooth. Pour over crust in pan. Sprinkle with pecans. Refrigerate while preparing cream cheese mixture.

• Combine cream cheese and sugar in large bowl. Beat at medium speed, scraping bowl often, until creamy. Add egg and vanilla, beating just until combined. Stir in sour cream by hand. Pour over caramel mixture.

• Bake for 35 to 40 minutes or until just set 2 inches from edge of pan. Cool on wire rack for 2 hours. Loosely cover; refrigerate at least 4 hours. Use foil to lift cheesecake from pan. Cut into 36 squares.

• Place cooling rack over large piece of waxed paper on counter. Combine chocolate chips and shortening in 1-quart saucepan. Cook over low heat, stirring constantly, until smooth (4 to 5 minutes). Pierce each cheesecake square with fork. Spoon chocolate over top and sides of each cheesecake square, letting excess chocolate drip back into pan. Place onto cooling rack. Let stand about 20 minutes or until chocolate is firm. Store refrigerated.

Sticky Date Cake

Preparation time: **15 minutes** | Baking time: **35 minutes** | **8 servings**

Cake

 1 (8-ounce) package chopped dates
 ½ cup boiling water
 ½ cup sugar
 ¼ cup LAND O LAKES® Butter, softened
 1 egg
 1 teaspoon vanilla
1¼ cups all-purpose flour
 1 teaspoon baking powder
 ¼ teaspoon salt

Sauce

 ⅓ cup LAND O LAKES® Butter
 1 cup firmly packed brown sugar
 ⅓ cup LAND O LAKES™ Heavy Whipping
 Cream

• Heat oven to 350°F. Place dates in medium bowl; add boiling water. Set aside.

• Combine sugar and ¼ cup butter in large bowl. Beat at medium speed, scraping bowl often, until creamy. Add egg and vanilla; continue beating until well mixed. Reduce speed to low; add flour, baking powder and salt. Beat until well mixed. Stir in date mixture until well mixed.

• Pour batter into greased 9-inch round baking pan. (Batter will be thin.) Bake for 35 to 40 minutes or until toothpick inserted in center comes out clean. Poke top of hot cake 10 to 15 times with fork.

• Meanwhile, melt ⅓ cup butter in 1-quart saucepan. Add brown sugar and whipping cream. Cook over medium heat, stirring occasionally, until mixture comes to a boil (3 to 4 minutes). Boil 1 minute.

• To serve, pour ¼ cup sauce over top of warm cake. Serve cake warm with remaining sauce, if desired.

Orange Nut Butter Cake

Preparation time: **30 minutes** | Baking time: **50 minutes** | **16 servings**

Cake

1 cup sugar

¾ cup LAND O LAKES® Butter, softened

3 eggs

1 tablespoon freshly grated orange peel

1 teaspoon vanilla

1 cup orange marmalade

3 cups all-purpose flour

1 teaspoon baking soda

½ teaspoon baking powder

½ teaspoon salt

⅓ cup orange juice

1 (5-ounce) can evaporated milk

1 cup chopped pecans or walnuts

Glaze

1 cup powdered sugar

1 tablespoon LAND O LAKES® Butter, softened

½ teaspoon freshly grated orange peel

4 to 5 teaspoons milk

• Heat oven to 350°F. Combine sugar and ¾ cup butter in large bowl. Beat at medium speed, scraping bowl often, until creamy. Continue beating, adding eggs 1 at a time, beating well after each addition. Reduce speed to low; add 1 tablespoon orange peel, vanilla and orange marmalade. Beat until well mixed.

• Continue beating, gradually adding combined flour, baking soda, baking powder and salt alternately with orange juice and evaporated milk, until well mixed. Stir in pecans.

• Spoon batter into greased and floured 10-inch Bundt® or angel food cake (tube) pan. Bake for 50 to 60 minutes or until toothpick inserted in center comes out clean. Cool in pan 10 minutes; remove from pan. Cool completely.

• Combine all glaze ingredients except milk in small bowl. Beat at low speed, scraping bowl often and gradually adding enough milk for desired glazing consistency. Glaze cooled cake.

Marble Sheet Cake

Preparation time: **25 minutes** | Baking time: **22 minutes** | **24 servings**

Cake

- 3 cups all-purpose flour
- 1 tablespoon baking powder
- ½ teaspoon salt
- 1¾ cups sugar
- ¾ cup LAND O LAKES® Butter, softened
- 4 eggs
- 1 tablespoon vanilla
- 1 cup milk
- ¼ cup unsweetened cocoa
- 3 tablespoons water

Frosting

- ½ cup LAND O LAKES® Butter, softened
- 3 cups powdered sugar
- ⅔ cup unsweetened cocoa
- 1 teaspoon vanilla
- 5 to 6 tablespoons milk

- Heat oven to 350°F. Grease and flour 15×10×1-inch jelly-roll pan. Set aside.

- Stir together flour, baking powder and salt in large bowl. Set aside.

- Beat 1½ cups sugar and ¾ cup butter in large bowl at medium speed, scraping bowl often, until creamy. Add eggs, one at a time, beating well after each addition. Stir in vanilla. Reduce speed to low. Add flour mixture alternately with 1 cup milk, beating well after each addition.

- Place 1½ cups batter into small bowl. Add remaining ¼ cup sugar, ¼ cup cocoa and water; stir until well mixed.

- Spoon three-fourths of plain batter into bottom of prepared pan. Spoon chocolate batter over plain batter. Spoon remaining plain batter on top, allowing some of chocolate batter to show through. Swirl two batters together gently with knife or spatula for marbled effect.

- Bake for 22 to 27 minutes or until toothpick inserted in center comes out clean. Cool completely.

- Beat ½ cup butter in medium bowl at medium speed until creamy. Gradually beat in powdered sugar, ⅔ cup cocoa, 1 teaspoon vanilla and 2 tablespoons milk. Continue beating, adding enough milk for desired spreading consistency. Frost cooled cake.

Southern Pecan Pie, p. 50

Fudgy Turtle Brownie Pie *(opposite page)*, p. 60

PIES &
TARTS

From the most simple, rustic crostata to the most complicated, elaborate tart, it is difficult to name another dessert quite as delightful as pie. Choose the flavor that is the perfect complement to your menu.

Key Lime Tart in Sugar Cookie Crust

Preparation time: **45 minutes** | Baking time: **15 minutes** | **12 servings**

Crust
- ⅓ cup sugar
- ½ cup LAND O LAKES® Butter, softened
- 1¼ cups all-purpose flour
- 1 tablespoon freshly grated Key lime peel*
- 2 tablespoons milk
- 1 teaspoon vanilla

Filling
- 1 cup sugar
- ⅔ cup Key lime juice*
- 1 tablespoon freshly grated Key lime peel*
- 2 eggs
- 4 egg yolks
- 6 tablespoons LAND O LAKES® Butter

Garnish
- 1 cup LAND O LAKES™ Heavy Whipping Cream
- 2 teaspoons freshly grated Key lime peel*

• Heat oven to 400°F. Combine ⅓ cup sugar and ½ cup butter in large bowl. Beat at medium speed, scraping bowl often, until creamy. Reduce speed to low; add flour, 1 tablespoon lime peel, milk and vanilla. Beat until well mixed. Press onto bottom and up sides of greased 10-inch tart or quiche pan. Bake for 15 to 20 minutes or until light golden brown. Cool completely.

• Meanwhile, combine 1 cup sugar, lime juice and 1 tablespoon lime peel in 2-quart saucepan. Cook over medium heat until sugar is dissolved (1 to 2 minutes). Reduce heat to low.

• Beat eggs and egg yolks in small bowl with wire whisk. Stir small amount of hot sugar mixture into egg mixture using wire whisk. Gradually stir egg mixture into hot sugar mixture. Continue cooking, stirring constantly, until mixture is thickened (6 to 8 minutes).

• Remove from heat. Stir in 6 tablespoons butter, 1 tablespoon at a time, with wire whisk. Cool 15 minutes.

• Pour cooled filling over crust; smooth top. Cover; refrigerate at least 2 hours.

• Just before serving, beat whipping cream in small bowl at high speed, scraping bowl often, until stiff peaks form. Place whipped cream in pastry bag fitted with large star tip. Pipe whipped cream onto tart; sprinkle with 2 teaspoons lime peel.

*Substitute regular lime peel and lime juice.

Southern Pecan Pie

Preparation time: **20 minutes** | Baking time: **50 minutes** | **8 servings**

Crust

- 1 cup all-purpose flour
- ⅛ teaspoon salt
- ⅓ cup cold LAND O LAKES® Butter
- 3 to 4 tablespoons cold water

Filling

- 1 cup light corn syrup
- ½ cup firmly packed brown sugar
- 3 eggs
- 2 tablespoons LAND O LAKES® Butter, melted
- 1½ teaspoons vanilla
- ¼ teaspoon salt
- 1 (4-ounce) package (1 cup) pecan halves

LAND O LAKES™ Heavy Whipping Cream, whipped, sweetened, if desired

• Heat oven to 375°F. Combine flour and salt in large bowl; cut in butter with pastry blender or fork until mixture resembles coarse crumbs. Stir in enough water just until flour is moistened. Shape into ball; flatten slightly.

• Roll out ball of dough on lightly floured surface into 12-inch circle. Fold into quarters. Place dough into 9-inch pie pan; unfold, pressing firmly against bottom and sides. Trim crust to ½ inch from edge of pan. Crimp or flute edge. Set aside.

• Combine corn syrup, brown sugar, eggs, butter, vanilla and salt in small bowl. Beat at medium speed, scraping bowl often, until well mixed. Stir in pecans.

• Pour pecan mixture into pastry crust. Bake for 50 to 55 minutes or until center is set. Cool completely.

• To serve, top each serving with whipped cream, if desired.

Apricot Raspberry Tart

Preparation time: **15 minutes** | Baking time: **38 minutes** | **8 servings**

Crust

1 (9-inch) unbaked refrigerated pie crust

Filling

1 (12.5-ounce) can almond filling

1 (15-ounce) can apricot halves, well-drained

1 (6-ounce) container (1 cup) fresh raspberries

1 tablespoon sugar

Garnish

2 tablespoons apricot preserves

LAND O LAKES™ Heavy Whipping Cream, whipped, sweetened, if desired

• Heat oven to 400°F. Press crust onto bottom and up sides of ungreased 9-inch round or 11×7-inch tart pan with removable bottom. Bake for 8 minutes.

• Spread almond filling evenly onto partially baked crust. Arrange apricots over filling; sprinkle with raspberries and 1 tablespoon sugar. Bake for 30 to 40 minutes or until crust is lightly browned. Cool completely.

• Place preserves in microwave-safe bowl. Microwave on HIGH for 15 to 30 seconds or until melted. Brush tart with melted preserves. Serve with whipped cream, if desired.

tip:

If canned almond filling is not available, make your own. Place 1 cup slivered almonds in food processor bowl fitted with metal blade. Cover; process until finely chopped. Add ¾ cup sugar, ¼ cup LAND O LAKES® Butter and 1 tablespoon all-purpose flour; process until well mixed. Add 1 egg, 2 tablespoons LAND O LAKES™ Half & Half and 1 teaspoon almond extract. Cover; process until well mixed.

Toasted Almond Tart

Preparation time: **40 minutes** | Baking time: **43 minutes** | **10 servings**

Pastry

  1 cup all-purpose flour
  ⅛ teaspoon salt
  6 tablespoons cold LAND O LAKES® Butter
  3 to 4 tablespoons cold water

Filling

  ⅔ cup sugar
  ½ cup LAND O LAKES® Butter, softened
  1 (6-ounce) package (1⅔ cups) sliced
    almonds, toasted
  2 teaspoons vanilla
  2 eggs

Topping

  1 cup LAND O LAKES™ Heavy Whipping
    Cream
  1 tablespoon sugar
  2 teaspoons amaretto liqueur*

• Heat oven to 350°F. Combine flour and salt in large bowl; cut in 6 tablespoons butter with pastry blender or fork until mixture resembles coarse crumbs. Mix in enough water with fork until flour mixture is just moistened. Shape into a ball.

• Roll out pastry ball on lightly floured surface into 14×9-inch rectangle. Place in ungreased 11×7-inch tart pan with removable bottom. Prick bottom of pastry with fork. Bake for 20 minutes or until pastry is light golden brown.

• Combine sugar, ½ cup butter, almonds and vanilla in large bowl. Beat at medium speed until creamy and almonds are broken. Add eggs; mix well.

• Spread almond mixture onto hot, partially baked pastry. Bake for 23 to 28 minutes or until filling feels firm to touch. Cool completely.

• Meanwhile, beat whipping cream in small bowl at high speed until soft peaks form. Add sugar; continue beating until stiff peaks form. Stir in amaretto.

• To serve, dollop each serving with flavored whipped cream. Store refrigerated.

*Substitute ¼ teaspoon almond extract.

tip:
Recipe can be made ahead, wrapped and frozen for several days, if desired. Top with whipped cream just before serving.

tip:
To toast almonds, spread evenly in shallow pan. Bake at 350°F, stirring once, for 4 to 6 minutes or until lightly browned. Cool completely.

Plum Crostata

Preparation time: **15 minutes** | Baking time: **40 minutes** | **10 servings**

Crust

- 2 cups all-purpose flour
- ¼ cup sugar
- ½ teaspoon salt
- ¾ cup cold LAND O LAKES® Butter
- 6 to 8 tablespoons cold water

Filling

- 6 medium (3 cups) ripe plums, pitted, sliced ⅛ inch thick
- ½ cup firmly packed brown sugar
- 1 tablespoon orange juice
- 1 to 2 teaspoons freshly grated orange peel
  Powdered sugar, if desired

• Heat oven to 400°F. Combine flour, sugar and salt in medium bowl; cut in butter with pastry blender or fork until mixture resembles coarse crumbs. Mix in water with fork until flour is just moistened.

• Press or roll pastry into 14-inch circle onto ungreased baking sheet. Shape into 10-inch circle by forming 2-inch rim around outside edge; loosely crimp edge. Prick bottom of pastry with fork. Bake for 15 minutes.

• Arrange plums in pinwheel fashion on pastry. Stir together brown sugar, orange juice and orange peel in small bowl; spread evenly over plums. Continue baking for 25 to 30 minutes or until pastry is golden brown.

• Just before serving, sprinkle with powdered sugar, if desired.

Caramelized Banana Tart

Preparation time: **15 minutes** | Baking time: **30 minutes** | **10 servings**

  3 tablespoons LAND O LAKES® Butter
⅔ cup sugar
⅓ cup pecan halves
  3 large firm bananas
  2 tablespoons lemon juice
½ (17¼-ounce) package frozen puff pastry, thawed
    Powdered sugar

• Heat oven to 425°F. Melt butter in 11×7-inch baking pan in oven; sprinkle evenly with sugar. Top with pecans.

• Cut bananas diagonally into slices. Place bananas over sugar, overlapping if necessary. Drizzle with lemon juice.

• Unfold thawed pastry; stretch or roll slightly to fit pan. Place pastry over bananas. Tuck edges of pastry in around edges of filling.

• Bake for 30 to 35 minutes or until pastry is golden brown and sauce is bubbly.

• Loosen edges of pan with spatula or knife. Carefully invert onto serving platter. Sprinkle with powdered sugar. Serve warm.

tip:
Make sure thawed puff pastry does not become warm or it may not rise properly. When rolling, work from center of dough toward edges taking care to keep consistent thickness.

tip:
If using a glass baking dish, reduce oven temperature to 400°F. Bake as directed above.

Double Berry Pandowdy

Preparation time: **20 minutes** | Baking time: **35 minutes** | **6 servings**

    2 cups blackberries
    2 cups raspberries
    1 cup sugar
 1¼ cups all-purpose flour
    2 teaspoons baking powder
  ¼ teaspoon salt
    3 tablespoons cold LAND O LAKES® Butter
  ⅓ cup buttermilk*
      1 teaspoon sugar

• Heat oven to 400°F. Combine blackberries, raspberries, ¾ cup sugar and ¼ cup flour in large bowl. Pour into ungreased 9-inch square (2-quart) baking dish.

• Combine remaining sugar, remaining flour, baking powder and salt in large bowl; cut in butter with pastry blender or fork until mixture resembles coarse crumbs. Add buttermilk; mix with fork just until dough forms a ball. Roll out dough into 9-inch square on lightly floured surface. Cut several slits in dough with sharp knife. Lay pastry gently over prepared fruit. Sprinkle dough with 1 teaspoon sugar.

• Bake for 10 to 12 minutes or until lightly browned. Reduce oven temperature to 350°F. Bake for 25 to 30 minutes or until golden brown and bubbly. Remove from oven.

• To serve, cut through crust with a fork to form pieces and push pieces of crust into the fruit or serve crust-side down. Serve warm or at room temperature.

*Substitute 1 teaspoon vinegar or lemon juice and enough milk to equal ⅓ cup. Let stand 10 minutes.

tip:

To help prevent dough from sticking, use a pastry cloth and rolling pin cover. A pastry cloth is a large canvas cloth on which pastry or dough can be rolled. A clean white dish towel may be substituted. A rolling pin cover is a stretchable "stocking" that fits over the rolling pin. Rolling out dough is much easier because the dough doesn't stick as readily to the flour-dusted fabric. Less flour is needed to prevent dough from sticking to the pastry cloth or rolling pin cover, keeping your pastry light and flaky.

Coconut Banana Cream Pie

Preparation time: **45 minutes** | Baking time: **29 minutes** | **8 servings**

Crust

  1 (7-ounce) package (2⅔ cups) sweetened
     flaked coconut
  ¼ cup LAND O LAKES® Butter, melted

Filling

  ½ cup sugar
  ¼ cup all-purpose flour
  ¼ teaspoon salt
  2 cups milk
  3 eggs, separated
  1 teaspoon vanilla
  1 medium banana, sliced

Meringue

  3 reserved egg whites
  6 tablespoons sugar

• Heat oven to 325°F. Reserve ¼ cup coconut. Set aside.

• Combine remaining coconut and butter in medium bowl; press onto bottom and up sides of ungreased 9-inch pie pan. Bake for 20 to 25 minutes or until golden brown.

• Meanwhile, combine ½ cup sugar, flour and salt in 2-quart saucepan; stir in milk. Cook over medium heat, stirring constantly, until mixture comes to a full boil (7 to 8 minutes). Remove from heat. Stir small amount of milk mixture into egg yolks; whisk egg yolk mixture into remaining hot milk mixture. Reduce heat to low. Cook, stirring constantly, until mixture reaches 160°F and is thick enough to coat the back of a metal spoon (1 to 2 minutes). (DO NOT BOIL.) Stir in vanilla. Pour half of hot filling into baked crust; cover with banana slices. Top with remaining filling.

• Increase oven temperature to 350°F. Beat egg whites in small bowl at high speed until foamy. Continue beating, gradually adding 6 tablespoons sugar, until glossy and stiff peaks form. Spread onto hot filling, sealing to edge of crust. Sprinkle with reserved coconut.

• Bake for 20 to 22 minutes or until meringue reaches 160°F and coconut is browned. Cool 30 minutes at room temperature. Refrigerate at least 3 hours. Store refrigerated.

Crumb Top Rhubarb Pie

Preparation time: **40 minutes** | Baking time: **50 minutes** | **8 servings**

Crust

     1 cup all-purpose flour
    ⅛ teaspoon salt
    ⅓ cup cold LAND O LAKES® Butter
     3 to 4 tablespoons cold water

Filling

    1¼ cups sugar
     3 tablespoons cornstarch
    ½ teaspoon ground cinnamon
    ¼ teaspoon ground nutmeg
     4 cups fresh rhubarb, sliced ¼-inch thick
    ⅔ cup chopped pecans

Topping

     1 cup all-purpose flour
    ⅔ cup sugar
    ½ cup cold LAND O LAKES® Butter

• Heat oven to 400°F. Combine 1 cup flour and salt in large bowl; cut in ⅓ cup butter with pastry blender or fork until mixture resembles coarse crumbs. Stir in enough water with fork just until flour is moistened. Shape into ball; flatten slightly.

• Roll out ball of dough on lightly floured surface into 12-inch circle. Fold into quarters. Place dough into 9-inch deep-dish pie pan; unfold, pressing firmly against bottom and sides. Trim crust to ½ inch from edge of pan. Crimp or flute edge. Set aside.

• Combine all filling ingredients except rhubarb and pecans in large bowl. Add rhubarb; toss until well coated. Spoon into prepared crust; sprinkle with pecans. Set aside.

• Combine 1 cup flour and ⅔ cup sugar in medium bowl; cut in ½ cup butter with pastry blender or fork until mixture resembles coarse crumbs. Sprinkle mixture over rhubarb. Cover edge of crust with 2-inch strip of aluminum foil. Bake for 50 to 60 minutes or until topping is golden brown and filling bubbles around edges. Remove aluminum foil during last 10 minutes, if desired.

Fudgy Turtle Brownie Pie

Preparation time: **20 minutes** | Baking time: **33 minutes** | 8 servings

Brownie

- 1 (19.4-ounce) package brownie mix with pecans
- 3 tablespoons water
- ½ cup LAND O LAKES® Butter, melted
- 2 eggs
- 12 caramels, unwrapped, cut in half

Sauce

- 15 caramels, unwrapped
- ⅓ cup real semi-sweet chocolate chips
- ¼ cup LAND O LAKES™ Half & Half

Topping

- 1 quart butter pecan ice cream, softened
- ½ cup chopped pecans, if desired

- Heat oven to 350°F. Grease bottom only of 9-inch pie pan. Set aside.

- Combine all brownie ingredients except caramels in large bowl; stir until well mixed.

- Spread batter into prepared pan. Place caramel halves evenly over batter; press down lightly. Bake for 33 to 38 minutes or until top is set and toothpick inserted 2 inches from side comes out clean. Score into wedges while warm. Cool completely; cut into wedges.

- Meanwhile, combine all sauce ingredients in 1-quart saucepan. Cook over medium heat, stirring constantly, until smooth. Cool 5 minutes.

- To serve, place brownie wedges on individual serving plates. Top with ice cream; drizzle with sauce. Sprinkle with pecans, if desired.

tip:
Refrigerate any leftover sauce; reheat before serving.

Yogurt Berry Pie

Preparation time: **25 minutes** | Baking time: **15 minutes** | **10 servings**

Crust

  2 cups vanilla wafer crumbs
  ¼ cup LAND O LAKES® Butter, melted

Filling

  1 pint fresh strawberries, hulled, chopped
  ⅓ cup sugar
  2 (8-ounce) containers vanilla or strawberry-flavored yogurt
  1 cup LAND O LAKES™ Heavy Whipping Cream

• Heat oven to 300°F. Combine all crust ingredients in medium bowl. Press mixture evenly onto bottom and up sides of ungreased 9-inch pie pan. Bake for 15 to 20 minutes or until crust is evenly browned. Cool 30 minutes.

• Combine strawberries, sugar and yogurt in medium bowl.

• Beat whipping cream in small bowl at high speed until stiff peaks form (3 to 4 minutes). Gently stir into strawberry mixture. Spoon strawberry mixture into cooled crust. Cover; freeze until firm (8 hours or overnight).

• Remove from freezer 30 minutes before serving. To serve, cut into wedges.

tip:

You can substitute other fruits for the strawberries and use a corresponding yogurt flavor in the recipe, such as raspberries and raspberry yogurt, or chopped fresh peaches and peach yogurt.

Chinese Almond Cookies, p. 76

Sugared Rum Balls (*opposite page*), p. 68

COOKIES & CANDIES

Bake up a batch of something sweet for someone special. Easy to make (and even easier to eat!), these sweet bites are the perfect little treats whatever the occasion or celebration or for no reason at all.

Double Chocolate Macaroons

Preparation time: **15 minutes** | Baking time: **11 minutes per pan** | **24 cookies**

Cookie

  4 egg whites
  2 tablespoons light corn syrup
  1 teaspoon almond extract
  3 cups sweetened flaked coconut
  6 tablespoons all-purpose flour
  ½ cup white baking chips

Drizzle

  2 (1-ounce) squares (⅓ cup) bittersweet baking chocolate, chopped
  ½ teaspoon shortening

• Line cookie sheets with parchment paper or aluminum foil. Spray with no-stick cooking spray. Set aside.

• Combine egg whites, corn syrup and almond extract in small bowl. Stir with fork until well mixed.

• Combine coconut and flour in large bowl; toss with hands until coconut is no longer lumpy. Stir in baking chips. Pour egg mixture over coconut mixture. Stir with rubber spatula until well mixed. Refrigerate 15 minutes.

• Heat oven to 350°F. Drop dough by heaping tablespoonfuls, 1 inch apart, onto prepared cookie sheet. Press firmly into mounds. Bake for 11 to 13 minutes or until golden brown. Let cool 5 minutes; remove from pan. Cool completely.

• Melt bittersweet chocolate and shortening in 1-quart saucepan over low heat; stir until smooth. Drizzle cooled cookies with melted chocolate. Let stand until chocolate is set. Store between sheets of waxed paper in container with tight-fitting lid.

tip:

To measure coconut, place coconut in large bowl. Separate lumps with hands. Place into measuring cups; do not pack.

tip:

Unopened coconut in plastic bags can be stored up to 6 months at room temperature. Leftover coconut can be stored in a container with a tight-fitting lid in the refrigerator or freezer.

Orange Espresso Spiced Nuts

Preparation time: **10 minutes** | Baking time: **25 minutes** | **5 cups**

    1 cup sugar
    1 tablespoon espresso powder*
    ¼ teaspoon ground cinnamon
    ⅛ teaspoon salt
    2 egg whites
    2 cups pecan halves
    2 cups lightly salted dry-roasted whole cashews
    1 cup walnut halves
    1 tablespoon freshly grated orange peel
    ¼ cup LAND O LAKES® Butter

• Heat oven to 325°F. Combine sugar, espresso powder, cinnamon and salt in small bowl.

• Place egg whites in medium bowl. Beat at high speed, scraping bowl often, until soft peaks form. Continue beating, gradually adding sugar mixture, until stiff peaks form. Gently stir in nuts and orange peel.

• Line 15×10×1-inch jelly-roll pan with heavy-duty aluminum foil. Melt butter in oven in foil-lined pan (4 to 6 minutes). Spread nut mixture over butter. Bake, stirring every 10 minutes, for 25 to 30 minutes or until nuts are browned and no butter remains. Cool completely. Store in container with tight-fitting lid.

*Substitute 4 teaspoons instant coffee granules.

tip:
Teachers, mail carriers and neighbors will appreciate these sweet-spicy nuts at holiday time. Just place the cooled nuts in a festive mug, cover with plastic food wrap and tie with holiday ribbon.

Sugared Rum Balls

Preparation time: **30 minutes** | **48 candies**

½ cup LAND O LAKES® Butter, melted
¼ cup rum*
2 tablespoons honey
2 cups crushed vanilla wafers
1 cup finely chopped pecans
½ cup sweetened flaked coconut
3 tablespoons unsweetened cocoa
    Sugar

• Combine butter, rum and honey in large bowl. Stir in vanilla wafers, pecans, coconut and cocoa until well mixed.

• Shape rounded teaspoonfuls of dough into 1-inch balls. Roll in sugar.

• Store refrigerated in container with tight-fitting lid up to 3 weeks. Roll in sugar again before serving. Serve in paper candy cups.

*Substitute ¼ cup water plus 1 teaspoon rum extract.

Saucepan Espresso Walnut Fudge

Preparation time: **15 minutes** | Cooking time: **8 minutes** | **3 dozen candies**

- ½ cup LAND O LAKES® Butter
- ⅓ cup LAND O LAKES™ Heavy Whipping Cream or Fat Free Half & Half
- 1½ cups real semi-sweet chocolate chips
- 1 tablespoon instant espresso coffee powder*
- 1 tablespoon vanilla
- 3 cups powdered sugar
- ¼ cup chopped walnuts or black walnuts

• Melt butter in heavy 4-quart saucepan over medium-low heat (3 to 4 minutes). Add whipping cream, chocolate chips and espresso powder. Continue cooking until chocolate chips are melted (5 to 7 minutes). Remove from heat; stir in vanilla. Add powdered sugar. Beat with a hand mixer at medium speed until well mixed.

• Line 8 or 9-inch square pan with aluminum foil. Butter foil. Spread fudge into prepared pan. Sprinkle with chopped walnuts; gently press nuts into fudge.

• Cover; refrigerate until firm (at least 2 hours). Cut into squares. Store refrigerated in container with tight-fitting lid.

*Substitute 3 to 4 teaspoons instant coffee granules.

microwave directions:
Combine butter, whipping cream, chocolate chips and espresso powder in large microwave-safe bowl. Microwave on HIGH, stirring once, until butter and chocolate chips are melted (2 to 2½ minutes). Stir in powdered sugar and vanilla. Continue as directed above.

tip:
If you love walnuts, stir an additional ¼ cup walnuts into fudge before spreading into pan and top fudge with additional walnuts.

Turtle Thumbprints

Preparation time: **20 minutes** | Baking time: **7 minutes per pan** | **4 dozen cookies**

Cookie

⅔ cup LAND O LAKES® Butter, softened
½ cup sugar
2 egg yolks
1 teaspoon vanilla
1½ cups all-purpose flour

Filling

20 caramels, unwrapped
2 tablespoons LAND O LAKES™ Heavy Whipping Cream
48 pecan halves

Drizzle

1 cup real semisweet chocolate chips
1 tablespoon shortening

• Combine butter, sugar, egg yolks and vanilla in large bowl. Beat at medium speed, scraping bowl often, until creamy. Reduce speed to low; add flour. Beat until well mixed. Cover; refrigerate until firm (at least 1 hour).

• Heat oven to 375°F. Shape dough into 1-inch balls. Place 1 inch apart onto ungreased cookie sheets. Make indentation in center of each cookie with thumb. (Edges may crack slightly.) Bake for 7 to 10 minutes or until edges begin to brown. Cool completely. Store cookies in a container with a tight-fitting lid for 2 to 3 days or freeze for up to 2 months.

• On serving day, combine caramels and whipping cream in medium microwave-safe bowl. Microwave on HIGH 1 minute; stir. Continue microwaving 1 minute or until melted; stir until smooth. Spoon about ½ teaspoon caramel mixture into center of each cookie. Top with pecan half.

• Place chocolate chips and shortening in small microwave-safe bowl. Microwave on HIGH 1 minute; stir. Continue microwaving 30 seconds or until melted; stir until smooth. Drizzle over cookie. Let stand until set (about 2 hours).

tip:
To store drizzled cookies, arrange between layers of waxed paper in a container with a tight-fitting lid. Store at room temperature for 1 to 2 days or freeze for up to 2 months

tip:
If caramel filling gets too thick, reheat in microwave for 10 to 15 seconds until it becomes spoonable again.

tip:
Place cookies on a cooling rack over a piece of waxed paper to catch any extra chocolate drizzle.

Glazed Lemon-Lime Ginger Cookies

Preparation time: **45 minutes** | Baking time: **7 minutes per pan** | **4 dozen cookies**

Cookie

1 cup LAND O LAKES® Butter, softened
¾ cup sugar
1 egg
1 tablespoon freshly grated lemon peel
½ teaspoon freshly grated lime peel
2¼ cups all-purpose flour
¼ cup crystallized ginger, finely chopped*
½ teaspoon baking powder
½ teaspoon salt
  Sugar

Glaze

1½ cups powdered sugar
1 teaspoon freshly grated lemon peel
½ teaspoon freshly grated lime peel
3 to 5 tablespoons lemon juice

• Heat oven to 375°F. Combine butter and sugar in large bowl. Beat at medium speed until creamy. Add egg, 1 tablespoon lemon peel and ½ teaspoon lime peel; continue beating until well mixed. Reduce speed to low; add flour, ginger, baking powder and salt. Beat until well mixed.

• Shape dough into 1¼-inch balls with lightly floured hands; roll in sugar. Place 1 inch apart onto ungreased cookie sheets. Flatten to 1½-inch circle with bottom of glass dipped in sugar. Bake for 7 to 10 minutes or until edges just begin to brown. Cool completely.

• Combine powdered sugar, 1 teaspoon lemon peel, ½ teaspoon lime peel and enough lemon juice for desired spreading consistency in small bowl. Spread about 1 teaspoon glaze over top of each cooled cookie; let stand until glaze is completely set.

*Substitute ⅛ teaspoon ground ginger.

tip:
The grated peel of one lemon or lime equals about 1 tablespoon.

Chinese Almond Cookies

Preparation time: **40 minutes** | Baking time: **11 minutes per pan** | **4 dozen cookies**

- 1 cup LAND O LAKES® Butter, softened
- ¾ cup sugar
- 1 egg
- 1 teaspoon almond extract
- 2¼ cups all-purpose flour
- 1 teaspoon baking powder
- ¼ teaspoon salt
- 48 whole blanched almonds
- 1 egg yolk
- 1 tablespoon water

• Heat oven to 350°F. Combine butter and sugar in large bowl. Beat at medium speed, scraping bowl often, until creamy. Add egg and almond extract; beat until well mixed. Reduce speed to low; add flour, baking powder and salt. Beat until well mixed.

• Shape dough into 1¼-inch balls. Place 2 inches apart onto ungreased cookie sheet. Flatten slightly; press almond into center of each cookie.

• Beat egg yolk with water in small bowl; brush cookies with egg mixture. Bake for 11 to 15 minutes or until just set.

tip:

Butter gives a rich flavor and slightly crisp texture in these cookies. Far more flavorful than the fortune cookie, keep them on hand, baked and ready, in your freezer. Serve after your favorite stir-fry meal along with sliced fresh fruit or a dish of sorbet.

Cappuccino
Brownies, p. 93

Malted Milk Bars
(opposite page), p. 86

BARS &
BROWNIES

These classic brownies and bars are as simple to whip up
by the batch as they are delightful to eat.

Creamy Lime Coconut Bars

Preparation time: **15 minutes** | Baking time: **31 minutes** | **48 bars**

Filling
1 cup lime juice
2 (14-ounce) cans sweetened condensed milk
1 teaspoon freshly grated lime peel
1 to 2 drops green food color

Crust
1½ cups all-purpose flour
½ cup sugar
½ cup slivered almonds, ground*
½ cup cold LAND O LAKES® Butter

Topping
½ cup sweetened flaked coconut

• Heat oven to 350°F. Combine all filling ingredients in large bowl; set aside. (Mixture will thicken slightly.)

• Meanwhile, combine flour, sugar and ground almonds in large bowl; cut in butter with pastry blender or fork until mixture resembles coarse crumbs.

• Pat mixture evenly into ungreased 13×9-inch baking pan. Bake for 16 to 18 minutes or until edges are lightly browned.

• Pour filling mixture over hot, partially baked crust. Sprinkle with coconut. Continue baking for 15 to 17 minutes or until filling is set. Cool completely. Cut into bars. Cover; store refrigerated.

*Substitute ½ cup finely chopped macadamia nuts.

Frosted Apple Cinnamon Bars

Preparation time: **30 minutes** | Baking time: **33 minutes per pan** | **48 bars**

Bar
1⅓ cups all-purpose flour
1 teaspoon salt
¾ teaspoon baking soda
1½ cups uncooked old-fashioned oats
¾ cup LAND O LAKES® Butter, softened
¾ cup firmly packed brown sugar
½ cup sugar
2 eggs
1 teaspoon vanilla
1 (10-ounce) package cinnamon-flavored
  baking chips*
1 medium (1 cup) apple, chopped

Frosting
3 cups powdered sugar
¼ cup LAND O LAKES® Butter, softened
1 (3-ounce) package cream cheese, softened
1 teaspoon vanilla

Ground cinnamon, if desired

•Heat oven to 350°F. Combine flour, salt and baking soda in medium bowl; stir in oats.

•Combine butter, brown sugar and sugar in large bowl. Beat at medium speed, scraping bowl often, until creamy. Add eggs and vanilla; beat until well mixed. Reduce speed to low; add flour mixture. Beat until well mixed. Stir in cinnamon chips and apple.

•Spread batter into greased 13×9-inch baking pan. Bake for 33 to 38 minutes or until toothpick inserted in center comes out clean. Cool completely.

•Combine all frosting ingredients in small bowl. Beat at low speed, scraping bowl often, until creamy. Spread over cooled bars. Sprinkle with cinnamon, if desired.

*Substitute 1 (10- to 12-ounce) package white baking chips and 1 teaspoon ground cinnamon.

tip:
Cut bars with a wet knife to get a clean edge.

Butterscotch Cashew Bars

Preparation time: **15 minutes** | Baking time: **20 minutes** | **36 bars**

Crust
1½ cups all-purpose flour
¾ cup firmly packed brown sugar
½ cup LAND O LAKES® Butter, softened
¼ teaspoon salt

Topping
¼ cup light corn syrup
1 cup butterscotch-flavored baking chips
2 tablespoons LAND O LAKES® Butter
1 tablespoon water
¼ teaspoon salt
1½ cups cashew halves and pieces

• Heat oven to 350°F. Combine all crust ingredients in large bowl. Beat at low speed, scraping bowl often, until mixture resembles coarse crumbs. Press crumb mixture onto bottom of greased 13×9-inch baking pan. Bake for 10 minutes.

• Meanwhile, place all topping ingredients except cashews in 2-quart saucepan. Cook over low heat, stirring constantly, until chips are melted and mixture is smooth (4 to 7 minutes). Stir in cashews until well coated.

• Spread cashew mixture over hot, partially baked crust. Continue baking for 10 to 12 minutes or until golden brown. Cool completely. Cut into bars or triangles.

Malted Milk Bars

Preparation time: **40 minutes** | Baking time: **18 minutes** | 36 bars

  1 cup all-purpose flour
  ¼ cup malted milk powder
  ¼ cup unsweetened cocoa
  ½ teaspoon baking soda
  ½ teaspoon salt
  ¾ cup LAND O LAKES® Butter, softened
  ½ cup firmly packed brown sugar
  ¼ cup sugar
  2 eggs
  2 teaspoons vanilla
  ¾ cup chopped malted milk balls

• Heat oven to 350°F. Grease bottom only of 13×9-inch baking pan.

• Combine flour, malted milk powder, cocoa, baking soda and salt in medium bowl. Set aside.

• Combine butter, brown sugar and sugar in large bowl. Beat at medium speed, scraping bowl often, until creamy. Add eggs and vanilla; continue beating until well mixed. Reduce speed to low; add flour mixture. Beat until well mixed.

• Spread batter into prepared pan. Bake for 18 to 22 minutes or until top is set when touched lightly in center. Remove from oven; sprinkle with chopped malted milk balls. Cool completely. Cut into bars.

tip:

Malted milk powder adds extra flavor to these chocolate bars. The powder comes from sprouted, dried and ground grain, usually barley. Its distinctive, slightly sweet taste complements the cocoa in the batter. Chopped malted milk balls reinforce the taste and add a decorative garnish. Look for malted milk powder with other packaged beverage additions such as sweetened cocoa mixes.

Fruit & Almond Bars

Preparation time: **20 minutes** | Baking time: **34 minutes** | **36 bars**

Crust

1½ cups all-purpose flour

½ cup LAND O LAKES® Butter, softened

¼ cup sugar

Topping

1 (7-ounce) tube almond paste

½ cup all-purpose flour

¼ cup sugar

¼ cup cold LAND O LAKES® Butter, cut into pieces

1 (10 to 12-ounce) jar (1 cup) orange marmalade or strawberry spreadable fruit preserves

½ cup sliced almonds

Glaze

⅔ cup powdered sugar

1 to 2 tablespoons milk

• Heat oven to 350°F. Combine all crust ingredients in small bowl. Beat at low speed, scraping bowl often, until mixture resembles coarse crumbs. Press crumb mixture onto bottom of ungreased 13×9-inch baking pan. Bake for 14 to 16 minutes or until edges are lightly browned.

• Meanwhile, crumble almond paste into same bowl. Stir in ½ cup flour and ¼ cup sugar. Cut in ¼ cup butter with pastry blender or fork until mixture resembles coarse crumbs; set aside. Spoon orange marmalade evenly over hot, partially baked crust. Sprinkle almond paste mixture over marmalade. Sprinkle with sliced almonds. Bake for 20 to 25 minutes or until topping is golden brown. Cool completely.

• Place powdered sugar in small bowl. Stir in enough milk for desired glazing consistency. Drizzle over cooled bars.

tip:

Almond paste is made from finely ground sweet almonds and sugar. It can be purchased in tubes or cans in the baking aisle of your grocery store. Often it will be located near the canned pie fillings.

Gingerbread Pumpkin Bars

Preparation time: **15 minutes** | Baking time: **25 minutes** | 48 bars

Bar

1½ cups sugar
 1 cup LAND O LAKES® Butter, softened
 ¼ cup mild-flavored molasses
2¼ cups all-purpose flour
1½ teaspoons baking soda
 1 teaspoon pumpkin pie spice*
 ⅓ cup uncooked quick-cooking oats

Filling

 1 (15-ounce) can cooked pumpkin
 ½ cup sugar
 2 (3-ounce) packages cream cheese, softened
 1 teaspoon vanilla
 1 teaspoon pumpkin pie spice*
 2 eggs

Drizzle

 1 cup powdered sugar
 1 tablespoon LAND O LAKES® Butter, softened
 ¼ teaspoon vanilla
 1 to 2 tablespoons LAND O LAKES™ Fat Free Half & Half or milk

• Heat oven to 350°F. Combine 1½ cups sugar, 1 cup butter and molasses in large bowl. Beat at medium speed until creamy. Reduce speed to low; add flour, baking soda and 1 teaspoon pumpkin pie spice. Beat until well mixed. Place ¾ cup mixture in small bowl. Add oats to ¾ cup molasses mixture; mix well. Set aside.

• Press remaining mixture into ungreased 15×10×1-inch jelly-roll pan.

• Combine pumpkin, ½ cup sugar, cream cheese, vanilla and 1 teaspoon pumpkin pie spice in medium bowl. Beat until well mixed. Add eggs; continue beating until well mixed. Spread mixture over crust to within ¼ inch of edge. Crumble reserved oat mixture over filling. Bake for 25 to 30 minutes or until topping is light golden brown. Cool completely.

• Combine powdered sugar, 1 tablespoon butter and vanilla in small bowl. Beat at medium speed, gradually adding enough half & half for desired drizzling consistency. Drizzle over cooled bars.

*Substitute ½ teaspoon ground cinnamon, ¼ teaspoon ground ginger, ⅛ teaspoon each ground nutmeg and ground cloves.

tip:
Store bars in a loosely covered container in the refrigerator. Bars are best made no more than 1 day ahead as the crust starts to soften from the pumpkin filling.

tip:
Looking for a fabulous pumpkin dessert? Cut bars into 12 servings; top with ice cream or whipped cream.

Peanut Chocolate Swirl Bars

Preparation time: **20 minutes** | Baking time: **20 minutes** | **36 bars**

½ cup LAND O LAKES® Butter
1¼ cups firmly packed brown sugar
2 eggs
2 teaspoons vanilla
1½ cups all-purpose flour
2 teaspoons baking powder
½ teaspoon salt
1 cup real semi-sweet chocolate chips
1 cup chopped salted peanuts

• Heat oven to 350°F. Melt butter in 3-quart saucepan over medium heat (3 to 5 minutes). Remove from heat. Stir in brown sugar, eggs and vanilla. Add flour, baking powder and salt; mix well. Gently stir in chocolate chips and peanuts.

• Spread mixture into ungreased 13×9-inch baking pan. Bake for 20 to 25 minutes or until center is firm to the touch. (DO NOT OVERBAKE.) Cool completely. Cut into bars.

Cappuccino Brownies *(photo on page 78)*

Preparation time: **20 minutes** | Baking time: **33 minutes** | **25 brownies**

Brownie
- 1 tablespoon instant espresso powder*
- 2 teaspoons hot water
- 1 cup real semi-sweet chocolate chips
- ½ cup LAND O LAKES® Butter
- 1 cup sugar
- 1 teaspoon vanilla
- 2 eggs
- 1 cup all-purpose flour
- ½ teaspoon baking powder
- ¼ teaspoon salt

Frosting
- 1 teaspoon instant espresso powder**
- 2 to 3 tablespoons milk or cream
- 2 cups powdered sugar
- ¼ cup LAND O LAKES® Butter, softened

Drizzle
- ⅓ cup real semi-sweet chocolate chips
- ½ teaspoon shortening

• Heat oven to 350°F. Combine 1 tablespoon espresso powder and hot water in small bowl; stir to dissolve. Set aside.

• Melt 1 cup chocolate chips and ½ cup butter in 3-quart saucepan over low heat, stirring occasionally, until smooth (4 to 7 minutes). Remove from heat; stir in espresso mixture, sugar and vanilla. Add eggs, one at a time, mixing well after each addition. Add flour, baking powder and salt; stir until well mixed.

• Spread mixture into greased 8-inch square baking pan. Bake for 33 to 38 minutes or until brownies just begin to pull away from sides of pan. (DO NOT OVERBAKE.) Cool completely.

• Combine 1 teaspoon espresso powder and 2 tablespoons milk in small bowl; stir to dissolve. Add powdered sugar and ¼ cup butter. Beat at low speed, scraping bowl often and adding enough milk for desired spreading consistency. Frost cooled brownies.

• Melt ⅓ cup chocolate chips and shortening in 1-quart saucepan over low heat, stirring occasionally, until smooth (2 to 4 minutes).

• Drizzle melted chocolate over frosting; swirl with toothpick or knife for marbled effect.

*Substitute 1 tablespoon instant coffee granules.

**Substitute 1 teaspoon instant coffee granules.

index